The Gates of the Kingdom

Part 1

by Colin Russell Baker

* * * * *

Contents

Coronation Day 7

The Night Before Brotherhood 13

Inner Chambers 21

Other Books by Colin Baker 31

❄ ❄ ❄ ❄ ❄

ISBN 10: 1922223972

ISBN 13: 978-1-922223-97-5

Published in Australia

Dedicated to the Great King,

our glorious Lord and Savior,

Yeshua the Messiah; Adonai

Kabod; the Lord of Glory.

* * * * *

'ȁ e Gates of the Kingdom' is a book series which will take you on a spiritual pilgrimage, exploring events where the realms of Heaven and Earth have touched.

ȁ is pilgrimage is through places which will often be foreign to you. ȁ e names of people, places, and relationship terms have been preserved in their original language so that you will get a sense of the cross-cultural context of this amazing story.

You will notice that the narrator speaks only in English, and that his paragraphs always appear indented for your convenience.

Some of the characters are a bit rough around the edges, and some speak with strange accents. ȁ ese a re n ot s pelling m istakes. I t w ill b e well worth the effort of getting used to 'reading what you see' with these fellas.

A l ine d ividing te xt i ndicates a s witching o f realms.

ȁ e Heritage Series consists of four parts...

The Gates of the Kingdom

~

A story of seed-time and harvest, of sprouting and blossoming, of bearing fruit with seed unto the fullness ... A Kingdom sown, a Kingdom reaped, a glorious Bride without spot or wrinkle, a matchless gift from a Father to a Son; bone of His bone and flesh of His flesh.

Heritage Series

Part 1: Seeds: Prologue:

Within the Father's Glory, Jesus Christ is King of Kings, and all things are perfect. The realm is vast. So vast that only the omnipresent One can comprehend her form for he alone saturates her history, 'past', present and 'future'. Other citizens of the realm can only navigate that which they have seen in the Spirit ... Limitless? ...Yes, yet not omnipotent.

Within this vast Heavenly maze of events lie those eternal sectors which mate to their finite counterparts in the temporal realm.

Like windows into time and space, one has been forever sealed; one can be seen and entered by the Sovereign and anyone he might send; another is a sector most glorious and full of gateways with many passing through from place to place.

Near the beginning of the second sector there is a gate. It is called the Zion Gate.

On a day very dark in the lower realm, the King of Glory appears at this gate in the Heavens with scepter and crown. He sits down on a pavement of deep sapphire.

He has by the Spirit, summoned one of the princes from among the sons of God and is in fact intending to summon the whole populace into his presence 'in the gate'.

Coronation Day

Out from a distant part of the realm, a young man of noble character appears. Tall and clean-shaven, he is dressed in rich ceremonial garments. There is a ring on his finger and a fine gold band around his neck. Approaching with an air of absolute confidence, he sits down with his Lord…

"Lord, what's your desire that of all the host of the redeemed, you should summon me sovereignly?"

"You know me well my brother. We meet so often, you and I, but not like this. It is usually a matter of deep calling to deep between us, but now it is I who have summoned you; for a purpose."

The King seemed almost distracted. To the young prince, it was obvious that the King beheld much, his eyes scanning vast reaches of time and beyond.

"Lord, show me your heart. I'm yours to command."

A silence … the King holding His thoughts upon something very distant.

"Observe the kingdoms of Adam's age my friend. Among all of these, can there be found any sign of life?"

Mal paused as he searched all the kingdoms of Adam's age for the tell-tale radiance of life[1].

"Lord…" He paused again, still searching, "There's none! …Just a faint glow from the Kingdoms of David and Solomon. And something … like a tiny beacon of light that keeps reappearing on the mountain."

"Even these are not the life we know. But they're the only signs in the darkness of all the kingdoms of man."

"As far as life goes, surely these are but the seeds of hope; signs of the inevitable end to the darkness of that age."

"You've seen well my brother, but I tell you, more than signs and hope have come out from those beacons. Those 'beacons', as you call them, have come out from our father's heart. They are his word in physical expression."

"Mal, by me, by his word, he creates."

Face to face: a glance. Eye to eye: a twinkling. And in a flash of light unseen, Mal knew, just an inkling of his Lord's desire. And his Lord could see that he knew.

---

1   Life: Hayyim; life (plural); the life of the Godhead. (A sharing together in glory.)

"That first light on the mountain Lord," his heart now pounding, sensing things glorious, "I felt there was something... something about it... that attracted me. It... it spoke to me! It seemed ... familiar."

"Yes, my brother. That's why I've called you out."

"You bear my image and you've been endowed with my likeness. I'm sending you to plant a seed of life; one that will cause our father's desire to be fulfilled and glory to abound. I'm sending you to plant an expression of me, right there, in the midst of the nations, at the very beginning of their sojourn in my garden."

The King exhorts His prince, and as He does, the pavement beneath Him rises to form a glorious sapphire throne.

"Your name is no longer Mal but Malki-Tzedek! You are a king of righteousness and you are a king of peace. The Royal Priesthood begins here and now in you my brother! In the darkness of that age, men shall begin to see me through you and at the appointed time, the brightness of your testimony shall announce my coming in the heavens."

Melchizedek turned, and upon his knees, bowed low. As he did, the King stretched out his scepter and, for one eternal moment, rested it upon Melchizedek's head. For just a second, Heaven seemed to blink as 'future' and 'past' intersected with the present, and another beacon appeared in the heavenlies for those of us who grope their way from marker to marker.

"I send you to plant an image of this mountain and of this kingdom there amongst the kingdoms of men. It is called Tzion, for it is a citadel that speaks of me, the Son of Man and of our brotherhood. Right there upon that mountain Mal, you became who you are!"

"Lord, shall I go alone for such a task as this? I don't want to fail you, my beloved. Shall I not take with me something of glory?"

"You do well to fear my friend, for within that sector my glory is hidden from the eyes of men. Guard your heart well. You know that even your brothers have fallen in that realm. And remember, I'll still be in you. I alone shall go with you."

"As for things glorious, I give you the bread and the wine. These are the symbols of our kingdom for they speak of my house and of my life. It is with these seeds that peace and righteousness are established. Build such a kingdom upon the mountain. Build it upon me."

"That mountain is yours, even as I am yours. Rule from there!"

"No man shall ever prevail against you my brother."

"Malki-Tzedek; receive your crown!"

With those words, the King of Glory took hold of His own Crown from upon His head and lifted it. As He did, His own Crown remained and an image of it came up in His hands. This He lowered onto the head of Melchizedek.

Instantly there was a rumbling in the pavement coming from somewhere in the far reaches of the sector. It seemed to reverberate through the assembled host like rolling thunder, as off into infinity shock became a great roar of exuberant joy.

Melchizedek rose from before the feet of the King of Kings and at His bidding turned to face the myriads; his brothers and sisters, tears streaming down his face. And on the face of the Lord, a grin, so contagious that it turned into a jubilation which redounded throughout the heavenlies.

Whoosh! …He was gone; cheers echoing still, even to this day, in realms unseen.

•••••••••••

And there in the gateway of the mountain, upon a pavement of ordinary stone, dwarfed in the shadow of a great ash tree, stood one lonely royal of the

Sons of God with a cup, a loaf, and a crown … and, if you look closely, a feint scar around his neck.

❊ ❊ ❊ ❊ ❊

The Gates of the Kingdom

~

*A story of seed-time and harvest, of sprouting
and blossoming, of bearing fruit with seed
unto the fullness ... A Kingdom sown, a Kingdom reaped, a glorious Bride without spot or
wrinkle, a matchless gift from a Father to a
Son; bone of His bone and flesh of His flesh.*

Heritage Series

The Night Before Brotherhood

It was the beginning of summer and the heat of the day had been intense upon the rocky outcrops of Arba[2]. Sarai had been content that afternoon to relax in the tranquilizing shade of the whispering she-oak beside the tent.

Stretched out on a huge grass mat, one elbow on a cushion, she tossed knuckle-bones with a giggly ten year old.

---

2   Arba: The region of Hebron (Kiriat-Arba) Named after Arba, the greatest of the giants, builder of Kiriat-Arba.

Thus distracted, she casually watched a young woman and her two companions approaching along a well-worn pad from the slope below. Trailing behind in the shimmering distance, she could just make out the servants with their donkeys.

Just as the girl entered camp Sarai rose to meet her and called out…

"Hagar! Hagar! Come, there's cool water in the goatskin by the trough. How did you fare at the tents of Eshkol? Did you get the wine? And what about the herbs for the master's broth, you know tonight is special?"

"Yes my lady, you know I always do well at the market."

"I just thought there may have been some problem with that blotch on the hind of the he-goat. You know how cunning those Emori' can be if they find an excuse."

"They are cunning my lady, but your servant is much more cunning than they. I rubbed it with white clay this morning."

"You've done well. Shevai can fetch your water. Come; tell me all the news from the market."

That evening, beginning at sunset, the celebration in the crowded camp of Abram had in fact been something special. The sound of dancing, cheers and laughter continued late into the night.

"When will they ever get to bed?" sighed Sarai, as she fell onto the couch in a most un-comely manner.

Abram rolled over, leaning upon his right elbow, a grin from cheek to cheek not entirely disguised by the whiskers of his years…

"Maybe when the dew of heaven falls upon them my precious, but I'm not sure they'll all make it back to their tents. Eli'ezer's boys were asleep on the ground when I left. I'd sure like to know how they make that wine."

"Today when the sun rises, you'll all become brothers. Maybe then they'll tell you their secret."

"I can't imagine any one of 'em ever doing that. But with their appetite for fresh meat, it doesn't really matter. I can see this relationship working out well for us all."

"Things have gone pretty well here already. Will it really make any difference when you mingle blood with them in the morning?"

"It's something us men understand my love. Trust me. You'll see. When men become brothers, it's different. They'll never tell us how they make their wine, but when trouble comes we'll stand by one another no matter what. It'll be a good alliance and a strong one."

"We shall call this place Hevron, (Alliance) for Elohim has inclined the hearts of the mighty ones toward us here …And given us a refuge from the kings!"

"Is it true then that the kings are afraid of those three?"

"I'm not sure that the kings are afraid of them. Kedorlaomer has already killed many of the mighty men in Ashtoreth Karnaim. But this I know, those three are afraid of no one. And you know; I feel the same way since Elohim spoke to me and promised this land to our descendants. If anyone wants to fight Avram, he will also have to fight Elohim. As for Aner, Eshkol and Mamre, we shall be brothers and we shall not live under the kings!"

"But my lord, from where shall come our descendants? You know that I can't … that we have never … been … fruitful."

Abram fell back into his pillow, throwing up his hands … and the sheet which he immediately tossed off…

"Woman; don't even think like that. 'Elyon has spoken. We must accept His word. Don't worry. It will happen."

"When you mingle blood with them, will you become a giant?"

"Don't be silly woman, you're trying to change the subject."

"I am not! I …I was just wondering; where will they cut you?"

"What? …Oh, we'll just make some little scars on our shoulders woman and rub them together. It'll be alright."

Sarai rolled over and put her arm around Abram's hairy chest, laying her head upon his shoulder.

"But my lord, there are three of them and you only have two shoulders, and besides, your shoulders only come up to their elbows."

Abram's brow furrows.

"Woman; just leave men's business to us men, and everything will be alright! …Okay!?"

"…If you say so my lord. I've heard from the market place yesterday that there's war coming. The kings are also making alliances. Is this true?"

"Yes woman. You amaze me. Nothing is hidden from you, is it?"

"You've not heard the half yet my lord. Many Emori' are moving up to the high place, to the Citadel of Peace. They're seeking refuge with their brothers the Y'vusi under Malki-Tzedek."

"That, my precious dove is in fact a very wise move. Maybe one day we might also see that city. In Y'vush, Malki-Tzedek has brought peace and led many to righteousness. I've heard that he actually possesses eternal life! Just imagine what an honor it would be to meet the Priest of 'Elyon."

"Yes my lord, but you won't believe what else I've heard from the market!"

"What?"

"That Malki-Tzedek is about to marry!"

"That! …Can't! …Be!"

Abram now sitting up on his couch, sober as a judge…

"Woman! …You can't just believe all the gossip you hear from the market! Who told you this?"

"Hagar told me. I asked her to catch up on things for me. I just…"

"Well it can't be true! Sarai! He's the Priest of Elohim. Not only that, he's like one who is Ben Elohim. He can't be killed. He's one who's already died! If he were to marry, the heir to the throne would be N'filim!"[3]

"Just think! What would happen to the priesthood! What would become of the Citadel! No! I will hear no more of it. You must not speak of this to anyone. Neither shall Hagar!"

"Too much of this kind of talk and we'll all be in trouble with Elohim. Where will our refuge be then?"

"I'm sorry. It sounded like good news to me."

"Well it's not! Now how am I ever gon'na get to sleep?"

"Don't worry my hero. I know how to take your mind off kings and things. Now come here."

With those words the lamp went out in the tent of Abram the Hebrew, shaded from the blazing moonlight by the great oaks of Mamre in Arba of the Ammorites, a land of giants and kings.

e Nephtilim were on the earth in those days … and also afterward … when the sons of God went to the daughters of men and had children by them. ey were the heroes of old, men of renown. (Genesis 6:4)

---

3   N'filim; Nephtilim; literal: 'The ones who have already died'; giants. (Named after the race of their fathers.)

The Gates of the Kingdom

~

A story of seed-time and harvest, of sprouting and blossoming, of bearing fruit with seed unto the fullness ... A Kingdom sown, a Kingdom reaped, a glorious Bride without spot or wrinkle, a matchless gift from a Father to a Son; bone of His bone and flesh of His flesh.

Heritage Series

Inner Chambers

From the tower of the fortress wall, Melchizedek looked up along the ridge to the great Ash-tree[4] or Araunah, which spoke to him in such inescapable tones of his sovereign place on the mount. Looking down across the valley his eyes find the place…

'Yes, just there. That's the place where off in the far distant future, Christ had agonized with His Father over Calvary.'

The warm, gusty air of the afternoon buffeted his face, ruffling his hair and stirring his spirit.

---

4   Ash tree: Rowan tree; also called Mountain Ash or Araunah in that region.

All appeared quiet in a land full of trouble and war but news of Mamre and his two brothers had already reached him. They had taken up arms with Abram, the friend of God, and gone in pursuit of Kedor-laomer for the sake of brotherhood. About nine hundred hot-blooded zealots; Hebrew and Amorite together, chasing an army of ten thousand warriors with the idea of taking their booty!

Melchizedek remembered well what the outcome would be. In fact, he had been waiting for this day. The passing on of the bread and the wine would be a momentous event not only in the age of man, but also to his own day and even to the age to come.

'Another marker shortly to appear in the Heavens,' he mused.

'Besides all this, Kedor-laomer was about to learn a lesson in tithing.' (He had rebelled against the law of the Valley of the King. Failing to acknowledge the sovereignty of Adonai, he had fled to the north.) 'More to the point, Kedor-laomer's master, one fallen arch-angel, would shortly be confronted by the Kingdom!'

Somewhere in the distance a shofar sounds, marking the setting of the sun. Turning to his right he glances across Jebus, just glimpsing the last pallid crest of it sinking into the dusty haze of

Canaan and, as was his custom at the beginning of each new day; he looks across to his chambers and is within them.

Sinking to his knees, he brings his spirit into the presence of the King who is enthroned within him, softly calling His Name…

"Jesus, Jesus!"

"Oh Lord. My precious Lord, surely this is my Gethsemane."

"What shall I do my King? My soul aches and wages war with the Spirit of life within me."

"I don't want to fail you Lord. How much longer shall I hold this feeble brotherhood, this 'Tzion' for the sovereignty of your name?"

"Guard your heart well my brother, guard your heart well!"

"Your words live in me always Lord and this is my testing; she doesn't understand. Truly your glory is hidden upon the face of this earth. My soul feints within me to see your glory. Yet Lord, you know how I've done all that you sent me to do."

"Lord, no-one sees your glory. They see only a king and priest, food, drink and a refuge from trouble. After the passing on, call me home, for I'm pressed beyond measure."

"Gat-Sh'manim[5] is a place my friend where a man faces separation because of love. It is a lonely place and it is a place that you've not yet fully known. Your heart gives you away my brother. The choice is yours. I recommend Gat-Sh'manim."

"And yes, you have finished all that I sent you to do, but you'll not be coming home until you've finished your course. It's your own destiny that demands you be pressed, as you say; 'beyond measure'."

"You've some distance to go Mal, but take courage, I will never leave you. Here on this mountain, you've planted righteousness and peace, but only deep travail will produce that kind of harvest in your own soul. The bread must be broken and the wine poured out."

"Look at the creation itself, how it travails to bring forth sons. Yet I tell you, it is not really the creation that travails, but the spirit of our father. Count the cost. Pay the price. Son-ship is worth any price and spiritual stature has a cost because it is of me."

"It is true that few see my glory in this age. It was the same for me right here in Yerushalayim and in the Galil. I spoke to open eyes. Some were opened

---

5   Gat-Sh'manim: Gethsemane; the place of travail.

many were not. I spoke the words of our father that they might hear. Very few did. That's not the point."

"Remember the word I gave to Yesha'yahu? ... 'Behold, a king shall reign in righteousness, and princes shall rule in judgment. And a man shall be as a hiding place from the wind; as a shelter from the tempest; as streams of water in a dry place; like the shadow of a great rock in a weary land. And the eyes of those that see shall not be dim, and the ears of those who hear shall listen.'"

"Here at the beginning we plant. At the end will come the harvest. Mal, we can't harvest what has not been sown. That which has been is that which shall be. Don't grow weary my friend. Now; come and see what I see…"

Melchizedek sensed the open air and a darkness – the sun had long set – and in the darkness the roar of rushing waters – the upper Jordan. Below him in the fields, between the ridge and the thicket; a sea of wailing humanity …Some were drunk, some crying, some groaning, others laughing … There were sheep and cattle, donkeys and camels.

On the far side of this pitiful hoard, to the north, four clusters of tents with blazing fires; the kings! Behind him, the hills had just begun to silhouette against the coming moon.

Melchizedek knew what would happen.

The moon had just begun turning silver as it climbed out of the dust and smoke that hung forever on the horizon of Canaan when the battle cry of Abram's coalition shattered the night. Hundreds of mighty men, great and small, broke into the camp on three sides.

Roaring like lions, they slew with unbridled ferocity every warrior on the edge of the camp. Charging forward toward the center virtually unopposed, they left behind a blood-spattered field of bodies, heads and limbs in their wake.

The forces of the kings attempted to make a stand in the center, but they were packed in so tightly with Abram's men pushing in on three sides that they were barely able to move let alone fight. The holler of men shouting and screaming filled the night air.

When they finally turned and ran north, the army of Abram could be seen scrambling over the dead bodies of their enemies, surging forward at an unrestrained pace.

The fires of the kings were snuffed out as men trampled both fires and tents, running in shear terror from their pursuers.

As the commotion receded there appeared out from the fellowship of the battlefield; a man, sword in hand, with a mighty one at his side, calling:

"Lot!" "Lot!" "Lot!" And, from among the freed ones, the reply: "Brother!"

Melchizedek was impressed.

"Lord, he's still mortal, yet he fights fearlessly, like a son of the Kingdom!"

"Yes," says the Lord, to Mal's eyes, that contagious grin again flashing across His face; "we can say that the strong man has met the Kingdom, and that he shall meet it again."

Melchizedek sensed a profound relief, like a load lifting off his shoulders.

"I promised him a seed Mal. That seed is me! By faith in me, he's overcome. He's waged war with the kingdoms of this world in the power of an indissoluble life and overcome them. And yes, except for my promise, he is still mortal."

"A bit like Simeon eh!"

"Yeah. A bit like Shim'on."

And looking up to the heavens, two stars announce the dawning; Melech and Zedek! Remembering his coronation and his Lord's words, Melchizedek is greatly encouraged.

And in the days of Amraphel king of Shinar Arioch king of Ellasar, Chedorlaomer King of Elam, and Tidal king of the nations, they made war with Bera king of Sodom, and with Birsha king of Gomorrah, Shinab king of Admah, Shemeber king of Zeboiim and the king of Zoar. All these were joined together to the valley of Siddim, which is the Salt Sea. They served Chedorlaomer for twelve years, and the thirteenth year they rebelled.

And in the fourteenth year Chedorlaomer and the kings that were with him came and struck the giants in Ashteroth Karnaim, and the Zuzim in Ham and the Emim in Shaveh Kiriathaim, and the Horites in their Mount Seir, as far as Elparan, which is by the wilderness. And they turned back and came to Enmishpat, which is Kadesh, and struck all the country of the Amalekites and also the Ammorites who lived in Hazazon Tamar.

And the king of Sodom went out, and the king of Gomorrah, and the king of Admah, and the king of Zeboiim, and the king of Bela which is Zoar.

Chedorlaomer, the king of Elam, and Tidal the king of the nations and Amraphel the king of Shinar and Arioch the king of Ellasar – four kings with the five.

And the valley of Siddim was full of asphalt pits and the kings of Sodom and Gomorra fled, and fell there, and they that remained fled to the mountain. And they took all the goods of Sodom and Gomorrah and all their food and went away. And they took Lot, the son of Abram's brother, and his goods and left; and he was living in Sodom.

And one who had escaped came and told Abram the Hebrew; for he was living among the oaks of Mamre the Amorite, the brother of Escol and Aner. And these had a covenant with Abram. And when he heard that his brother was captured, even then he led out his trained men, born in his household, three hundred and eighteen. And they pursued as far as Dan.

And he divided against them by night; he and his slaves and he struck them, and chased them as far as Hobar, which is on the left of Damascus. And he brought back all the goods, and also brought back his brother, and also the women and the people.

And the king of Sodom went out to meet him, after he returned from smiting Chedorlaomer and the kings which were with him, to the valley of Shaveh, it being the valley of the king (...the arena of the victorious king).

And Melchizedek king of Salem, brought out bread and wine; and he was the priest of the most high God. And he blessed him and said. Blessed be Abram of the most high God, possessor of Heaven and earth; and blessed be the most high God, who has delivered your enemies into your hand. And he gave him a tithe of all.

At this, one very angry fallen-angel closed his eyes, put his hands over his ears, and with a look of sheer torture on his face cried 'NOoo!'

And the king of Sodom said to Abram. Give me the persons and take the goods for yourself.

Unseen, but not entirely unheard, from somewhere near the shoulder of the king of Sodom their tortured spectator mutters through clenched teeth: "You fool! The people are the goods, my goods, and I will have them yet!"

And Abram said to the king of Sodom. I have lifted up my hand to Jehovah, the most high God, the possessor of Heaven and earth, that I will not take from all that is yours, from a thread to a shoe latchet, and that you may not say, I have made Abram rich. Nothing for me; only what the young men have eaten, and the portion of the men who went with me; Aner, Eshcol and Mamre; let them take their portion. (Genesis 14)

www.colininthespirit.com

Other Books by Colin Baker

from à e Voice Series:

The Voice in Galatians

The Voice in Thessalonians

The Voice in 1 Corinthians

...with more to come.

from à e Gates of the Kingdom Series:

The Gates of the Kingdom Part 2

The Gates of the Kingdom Part 3

The Little Gate of the Great King

...with more to come.

These titles and more are available in PDF, ePub and Audio format for Laptop, Tablet and Mobile devices from ***www.colininthespirit.com***

✻ ✻ ✻ ✻ ✻

About the Author

Colin Baker lives in Australia's Northern Territory in the remote Aboriginal Homeland Community of Gäwa.

Gäwa is a name well loved. It's origins are Macassan. It means 'Land of the King'.

His experience at Gäwa has been one of pioneering and gate-keeping, perseverance, patience and overcoming.

He is committed to the glory of God as is reflected in his vision to facilitate an embracing of the Gospel of the Glory by God's people.

His m andate i s pi ctured i n E zekiel chapter one when viewed in the light of the fact that 'movement in the Spiritual Realm is by vision'. ...And that the L ord's C ommunity i s t he v ehicle that transports the throne and the One seated upon it into all the Earth.

....

*Published by Kingdomgates Publishing
in the Northern Territory of Australia.*
www.kingdomgatespublishing.com.au

Other Copyright:

* * * * *